FOUR LOST CHILDREN

JOANNE BARD

Paperback: 978-1-961438-56-9
eBook: 978-1-961438-57-6
Library of Congress Control Number: 2023914395

This book is a work of non-fiction.

Ordering Information:

Prime Seven Media
518 Landmann St.
Tomah City, WI 54660

Printed in the United States of America

Table of Contents

My Inner Strength

In my words I sense a healing grace, for I have stepped into a saving place.

My thoughts expressed in sad confusion, leading me to no conclusion.

Many answers I do seek, unanswered questions my heart does speak.

Penning my thoughts is a special gift, helping those hollow feelings to lift.

So deep a loss I have known, the hurt I bare I have shown.

Down within my heart and soul, lives the wonder of my future role.

Answers that may never come, I may be the only one.

To heal the crime against my childhood losing a mother due to hate,

It would become my fate.

I speak to her. To let her heal, the deep emotions of anger I feel.

Let love flow in and out, let my body heal, I'm special no doubt.

Of my life I have control, believe me I have a beautiful soul.

Shannon Schram
Copyright 2022

Chapter One

It was snowing. The wind chill was rather cold on the hands if not completely covered. This was not unusual for Bridgeport, Ontario. Most people scarcely acknowledge the weather however on February 9, 1962 it was cold enough that some cars were stalled along the roadways with people frantically trying desperately to make it to work on time. It was a normal day in the Schickler household. Mom and dad had already left for work, dropping my brother Ken and younger sister Lee to the sitter's while my older brother and I rushed to get ready for school. It was a 3 mile walk in the bitterly cold weather. After what we called a hard day at school, my brother Steve and I were the first to arrive home. Mom and dad would return after collecting our younger siblings. Today though would be totally different, and the aftermath would leave scars on each one of us and change our lives forever.

It was a two bedroom shack we called home and was situated behind a house owned by Frieda Schantz. At one time it had been a chicken coop, but it had been totally remodeled into a two bedroom house. My mother worked with Frieda at the Hager Hinge Ltd. a factory not too far away. In the morning they would leave together, usually in a hurry. Today, though, would be different.

Steve and I arrived home from school as we normally did, this time to find our mother sitting at the kitchen table drinking coffee, crying and writing a letter. There was a vial beside her. We would learn the importance and the role that vial played, and why I have written this book. As my brother and I stood in front of her confused, I remember asking mom, "Why are you crying?" She spoke in a soft voice and said go to the house in front and we proceeded to do what we were told and left for Frieda's home. Several hours passed when my father staggered home with our younger siblings when I ran out to greet him and said daddy mommy is in the house crying." He replied, "go back into Frieda's house," so I did. It seemed like hours passed when the yard filled with police cars, ambulances and a few of our relatives. I guess it must have been at least an hour or two before we saw further activity, then suddenly I saw them take my mother out on a stretcher, and as I peered out the window tears streaming down my face, mom said," everything will be alright Joey". Even as I was crying, I desperately wanted to believe those four little words to be true. All I know is, this would be the last words my mother would ever say to me. Now that was how I remembered it as a 7 years old. Could it be that I forged a scenario in my mind that was not there or happened? Not sure.

After the ambulance left carrying our mother away, our grandfather on my dad's side of the family collected us four children, Steve 8, Joanne7, Kenneth 5, and Lee 4 to spend the night with him. Our father on the other hand was taken into custody for questioning about what had transpired that day and evening. It would be a husband/father's worst nightmare. Once we got to grandpa's house he asked us to get ready for bed. We would all sleep together in a big bed. Steve, Ken, myself and Lee. I guess deep down inside Steve and I knew we had to take care of the younger two. I remember trying desperately to get my sister to stop crying, as grandpa yelled out," If you don't stop crying, I will give you something to really cry about". That is when I came to the realization that our grandpa was not a patient man and could be extremely cruel, especially when there are four children down the hall scared, confused and very much alone with no one to comfort us, even if it was a hug or a few words of comfort, like, everything will be fine, would have been nice. We had to solely depend on each other to muster up enough strength to just make it through the night, so we held each other tight and cried ourselves to sleep. I remember my last thought as I drifted off to sleep, hoping we would awake and it would all just simply be a dream. It was not. We would all have our own little nightmare in our dreams for a long time to come.

Chapter Two

When we woke the next morning we were asked to go downstairs to the recreation room where our father was waiting. It was a large room with animal heads on the wall in a cozy atmosphere. I never liked the room much, being an animal lover and all, so to me and as a child, I thought it was cruel. Animals are the most beautiful creatures that were created, they don't deserve to be trophy's on someone's wall. As I glanced to my left I noticed my father sitting alone on the couch. He called us to come over to him. I remember how happy I was to see him. Dad lined us up in front of him and proceeded to say the words I wanted him to take back. He looked at us and said I have something to tell you, your mother is dead. The News hit me like lightning striking my heart and my knees began to buckle. What were those words again? Please tell me she's alright and coming home. The words kept pounding over and over in my head. She's gone never to return again. It would haunt me for the rest of my life. One question remained: Why? I would search a lifetime just to have that one word question answered. I desperately needed to understand so I could let it register in my mind maybe searching for the possibility that the pain would lesson, the broken heart could not just shatter, the confusion could begin to make some sort of sense out of this horrible tragedy, but most of all the loss of a beautiful human being not so great. There would be no more hugs or kisses, No holding her hand, no special moments together. Soon the smell of her perfume will be a memory and soon gone in such a short period of time forgotten. Her smile would fade and her laughter never to be heard again forgotten. I will never see her dance so beautifully and sing like an angel.

It would remain deep inside my consciousness until we meet again one day.

I Guess no one could have known the battle she fought deep down inside. I guess she lost. Mom would take a child with her that night. She was 3 months pregnant. The loss doubled in less than a few hours. The challenge was yet to come for her children. Later on in life the quilt, pain and confusion would consume me and always will. Why couldn't I have helped her? If only I would have come home sooner. It was the greatest loss in my life. The only thing I can do now is to try and go on without my mentor, my best friend, my world.

In the days that followed, I would watch as each of our siblings were sent off to live with our relatives, My older brother and younger sister would grieve together in the home of the one true person I have held responsible for my mother's untimely death, her mother, mommy dearest. Ken off to our Uncle Jack and myself to Uncle

Lloyd, both brothers on my father's side. Ken and I would grieve alone. In the meantime though, our dedicated and loving father decided to move on without us. We lost both parents in less than a few days. A grown man with a loss such as my mother is something I can comprehend, but abandoning four children under the age of 8 after a trauma we had all suffered, is downright unforgivable. I found myself asking that same question once again, why? Your children are filled with fear, loneliness, pain and confusion, the one and only person who should be there to comfort us, not tear us apart more than we already were, to vanish without a goodbye, gone in a flash. Two structures in our world collapsed in front of us and we were left to try and deal with two losses. The love we thought we once knew was gone never to feel it again. His after-save scent would fade as my mother's perfume. Never to hug, never to kiss, gone. It would remain that way for me for four years.

Chapter Three

Guelph, Ontario was not a large town compared to the surrounding cities like Kitchener, London, or Toronto. Alfred Harold Bard and Ivy Dennis would marry sometime in the early 1900's. This marriage would be based on deception. Ivy would tell Alfred she was pregnant with his child to trap him. Back in those days, unlike today, the man would marry her to avoid scandal. Her mother Kathleen Dennis had strong beliefs that a woman must be proper at all times. Her morals were so strong that after her husband George had an affair, she sent him packing and would never marry again. Sometimes when someone portrays you, they never learn to trust again. She was just that sort of woman. She would raise her children herself with financial help from her husband whom I never had the chance to meet. I wanted to see who made this woman so strong.

It didn't take Ivy long to conceive, she was in a hurry if she wanted her lie to remain secret, and a beautiful baby girl would be born on May 29, 1934. They name this little angel Joan Beatrice Bard. It was a happy occasion in the Bard family bringing home this bundle of joy, but it would become short lived. The next chain of events would destroy the lives of many families in the future. Ivy could be happy to stay home and care for Joan while Alfred struggled to work and provide for his new family. Everything appeared to be perfect for the new couple at least from the outside looking in but trouble was brewing in their marriage and how can it not when it was never based on love in the first place

Alfred started his career as the friendly neighbor milkman who went door to door providing a wonderful service to many of the people on his route. One night after his last delivery, when he got home he found out he would be a dad again. Alfred was delighted at the news of another addition, but also a little apprehensive that there would be another mouth to feed. A one family income is not easy at the best of times, not much different from today. He worried whether or not they could afford to raise another child. The next day he awoke to his everyday routine and scurried out the door to work but not before kissing his wife and little girl goodbye. Today would be different and no one could have known how this day would change and destroy that family apart.

As Alfred heading on his way to the first house on his route to deliver milk he tripped over the fence and broke his leg. In today's world we have compensation, but back then there was nothing available. His greatest fear flashed right in front of him. How on earth will he provide for his new family if he's out of work for 6 months and depression sank in and he started to drink to comfort himself and to forget about the problems which lay ahead of him. He started to separate himself from the family he was once proud of and his responsibilities hoping things would get better in the morning. Nothing like a good drinking spree with all hope is gone. He must come up with an alternative to make some money. He went to the local pub where he met up with some friends. They too were down on their luck. They weren't close or anything, just conversation. This relationship would change. As they drank beer after beer, they came to realize in a drunken stupor, they were in the same position and the wheels of stupidity would turn.

As they continued to drink, a plan would revolve to solve their financial burden, they would rob the Fergus Bank in Fergus, Ontario where they resided. Now no one in their right mind should be as crazy as that while consuming alcohol. Unfortunately to them it was the best solution to all of their troubles. They would spend days chasing the bank until they could draw an exact replica of the inside of the bank and the best time to put their plans into reality. The map was kept on Alfred's kitchen table. Little did he know, one of the men backed out of the scheme and went to the police to report the conspiracy to rob the bank as the officer's listened with amazement to the snitch, they decided to pay a surprise visit to Alfred's home and a surprise it was Alfred was unable to remove the map. He was then arrested and charged with conspiracy to commit a robbery and was sentenced to 3 years in prison. His pregnant wife and daughter will have to try and move on with their lives.

Chapter Four

Anna would now have to find another source of income to raise her little girl and the growing baby inside her now that her husband would be gone for three long years. She was nearing her due date and fear started to control her. The next steps to her pitiful life would affect one's around her. She came to a decision to aboard her baby by sticking knitting needles up her vagina and went into labor. The baby boy died shortly after. She had murdered her own son. He would become John Bard., Joan's only sibling. There was absolutely no remorse. Joan would remain a only, lonely child. In fact her life would become one disappointment after another.

Soon after that event, Anna would fall in love with a military man. The relationship started to unravel when he gave her an ultimatum, me or the child. Unfortunately her little girl would have to go. Anna packed up her daughter's belongings and dropped her off at her grandmother's home. She had such a tremendous loss of her father, brother and her mother in such a short time. So much pain and confusion, wanting to try and understand what is happening, or what had she done to be tossed away so easily. She was left with unanswered questions, and if the question was answered she was too young to process the information.

As for mommy dearest, she would love her military man not for long after the ultimatum, that would not be the last man in her sad and disgusting life. She would move from one man to another and be labeled the military camp tramp. Anna would continue to disgrace her entire family until she found the man with whom she could control and manipulate. She finally found him. His name was Paul who was a kind and loving man who worked all his life. Soon after they were married, Ivy cut him off from sex. Paul had his room upstairs with just a bed and dresser. He would have a bucket to relieve himself at night so she would not be disturbed. I remember us children laughing heartlessly every time we heard him use it. It would take years before we would actually feel disgusted by the ill treatment and embarrassment he had to endure his entire life.

Pault was given a small allowance to cover his tobacco and rolling papers. He was not allowed to purchase tailor made cigarettes, he would have to roll them. He would have to cook his own supper and make his own lunch while she sat around doing nothing but getting fatter and lazier as time went by, if that was possible. As a child watching this happen and to this day, I cannot fathom why Paul would tolerate his wife abusing him in such a degrading way. She would drain the life out of this kind soul and feel absolutely no shame let alone quilt.

Meanwhile, Joan was still in the care of her grandmother who simply adored her. After Her father Alfred served his prison sentence he contacted his daughter's grandmother asking how she was doing. The part that breaks my heart was that he chose to do it at a distance. Katheleen would tell him she was adjusting and coping, the best that she can. Alfred would not contact his daughter again until her wedding day. His excuse was he did not want to turn her life upside down, did I hear that right? Turn her life upside down? I think he had already completed that task too many years earlier. He believed he was about to complicate her life anymore then it was, so sentimental don't you think? I can be sure of one thing, I do not believe my mother would agree. You grow up all your life thinking adults are right, after all they are supposed to be a little more intelligent, then, the child before them. Well I'm here to tell you that sometimes adults should step back and allow the child to decide what is in their hearts and mind, then and only then, can the pain and confusion take the right path to start the healing. After all, we learn how to trust and respect others through our elders. When something as senseless and heartless as this starts down on the wrong track, it does not just affect one person, it is carried on through the family for generations to come. I would grow up calling this a bad seed. Unfortunately, I was right. You make mistakes or bad decisions because that is all you know and were taught. My mother never stood a chance, as doomed from the time she was conceived. They say you cannot love someone if you do not love yourself. I really hate to disagree. How can you love anyone let alone yourself unless you have been loved through your childhood? You can look up the definition in the dictionary, but if love was never felt in your life, then the meaning means nothing. A different language if you will. That is the devastating part, because the world is lost without love and so are a lot of innocent children.

Joan's grandmother would continue to raise her even though mommy dearest married Paul. I'm sure he could have adored her if given a chance. Instead she would adopt a little girl named Jane who would become more important to Anna then her own daughter. I will never forgive her for that. She also adopted a little boy named George I guess to replace the son she purposely aborted many years ago. Guilty conscience I doubt it. It was just another slap in the face to my mother. The hurt inside her must have torn her apart. The constant pain of knowing her mother not only chose a man over her, but a daughter and an unrelated brother. What a way to lose sight of your own identity and the feeling of wondering just where I fit in the scheme of this. Stripping her of herself. Joan would learn how to hurt in silence. She would take all that pain and sorrow with her to her grave. Such a waste to go through your childhood and a portion of your adult life feeling, lonely, unwanted and especially unloved. What is life without those three things,....you need them to survive? The emptiness that remains deep down inside you will never fill with life's greatest pleasures.

Chapter Five

Joan's grandmother did a wonderful job raising her especially without any assistance from her daughter or Joan's father. She was a strict but strong woman with beliefs of the olden days. She would teach her manners, how to walk, how to eat, and set the table. She would teach her proper cleansing and how important it is to always act like a lady. She would take her to Church every Sunday and help her with her homework. Joan would blossom into a prim and proper young lady. Grandma could teach her a lot of things, but something that she could not teach her sadly was her confidence, to trust the people around her. No one would begin to know the amount of pain she carried deep inside her heart and it hurt grandma to see it a great deal, for she couldn't do one thing and that was to erase her pain away.

Her granddaughters pain away. Joan was able to mask it well though, not showing the hurt that was eating at her day by day. No one can be trusted, after all she witnessed that once before. Everyone leaves you at one point in your life and for some a few times. Pain is such a funny thing to completely understand, first it is a burning sensation deep down in your heart and once it begins to heal it becomes one of life's scars and it will never go away. It just flares up from time to time throughout your life and starts the process all over again.

Joan would have contact with her biological mother, but it was far from a mother/daughter relationship. As far as she was concerned her grandmother was the mother in Joan's life and that would never change. Joan was respected by her whereas mommy dearest berated her all the time. Joan tried her best to be a good student in school.

She completed her grade 9 in Guelph, Ontario. She was an average student, but extremely shy. It was hard to make friends but she tried. She was a beautiful blond woman who carried herself well. Joan would make a man look twice at her. Not only did she have her outer beauty, she had it inside as well. She could light up any room, her beauty captivating everyone around her. One of her favorite songs was Cry by Johnny Ray. She loved to sing and dance. She would be singing to the radio as she danced delicately in the living room. Grandma would sneak into the room as she watched her dance and was amazed by her gracefulness with every step and sing with such passion. Joan would sing certain songs with so much passion you could feel the pain she had hidden deep inside her heart.

As Joan continued to mature, the boys started calling on her and grandma would have her hands full. She would have the biggest challenge of all and that was to see that no man would take advantage of her precious granddaughter.

Everything her grandma taught her was respected and it would break Joan's heart to ever let the only person she truly loved and trusted down. She could always count on her no matter how big or small the problem was.

Grandma would have strict rules when dating, grandma would demand to meet each young man and have a lengthy conversation with them first before she could leave. She would, with friends, go to the skating rink nearby every weekend. There was a young, handsome man named Bill who she was taken with. Bill was handsome, smart and extremely funny. Joan was so excited when he finally asked her out on a date. She would tell him he had to meet her grandmother first. It was her golden rule.

There would be several men who seemed to take an interest in this blonde beauty, but there was one amongst them all that stood out the most. His name was William John Schickler. He seemed to be the only one who could charm his way into her grandmother's heart and succeed. Bill and Joan would become the most beautiful looking couple amongst their friends. They would date just over a year when grandma asked Bill what his intentions were. That is when he asked her grandmother for Joan's hand in marriage. Grandma delightedly said yes of course, now it was time to find out what Joan would say. William and Joan became husband and wife on September 27, 1952 in Guelph, Ontario.

Chapter Six

William John Schickler was born August 26, 1932 in Kitchener, Ontario. He was the proud son of Albert and Clarissa Schickler. Bill would be the third son following Lloyd and Jack. A younger sister Shirley would be born two years later. William and Shirley would become extremely close compared to the other brother's. They would become the rebels of the Schickler family and would endure a great deal of pain and suffering in the not so far future. All in all they seemed to be a very happy family. I'm sure they had difficulties, what family didn't. Grandpa drank a lot, but kept a fulltime job as a truck driver in the City of Waterloo, Ontario. It must have been difficult to support such a big family.

But he was extremely strict and the children knew not to make any waves. My father Bill would tell me years later that grandpa would beat his children, but no one else in the family could back up that statement. I think it was an excuse for his behavior.

Grandma would stay home and care for the children. I am sorry to say I never had the pleasure of meeting this incredible woman. She would pass on October 10, 1954 months after holding me for the first time. Cancer would be the disease that would take her life. It must have been difficult for grandpa to watch cancer drain the life from her body day by day with a debilitating feeling of helplessness. So he continued to remind her of how much he loves her and if God was willing, He would trade his life for hers.

Bill as he was known by many was an extremely smart young man as well as a wise ass. He believed his humor and charm would get him out of situations he should not have been in. His grades were above average and went on to complete his grade 10 at Kitchener Collegiate Institute. He was quite popular amongst the students and had no trouble making friends. He was handsome and a bit of a class clown who craved all of the attention from those around him. He could charm himself out of anything, a lady's man. He could draw people to him young or old. In fact, later on in life, he would still have that talent. People admired him and wanted to be like him as if he was a celebrity, even with his poor impersonation of Elvis Presley and John Wayne. He was not talented in that area, but people did not care, being near him was worth the dry humor and sometimes condescending insults. He would use these vices to shield all of his own pain and suffering and teach his children to do the same. I am not sure to this day who my father truly was, I guess I will never truly know. You would have to strip him of his poor humor and impersonations to find his lonely soul. Then and only then, I believe there just might be a good and decent man trapped inside screaming to get out. This poor soul, in my mind, finds it easier to be someone else than himself. Forgive me for reminiscing but this just took me back into the first few chapters that I referenced the popular saying that you can't be someone unless you love yourself.... I believe in my heart my father was one of the unfortunate souls and I find this to be very sad, for he missed out on one of the best things life has to offer. He now only exists.

As Bill matured, so did his looks becoming more dashing to all the ladies near and far. He was a fantastic dancer which was one of his finest attributes. Bill knew how to dazzle the ladies, with a song, a little charm and dance. He was always the clown at the party, needing to be the center of attraction, sad really, but that was Bill. Maybe it stemmed from competing with two older brothers and maybe why his sister Shirley and Bill were close. No one will ever know for sure. He tried out in boxing, lightweight. He did not continue for long. Maybe it was the beatings he endured, or just was not good enough, only he knows why. To this day, I wonder if that is where all his anger came from. Did boxing turn this handsome charming man into a monster later on in life?

After boxing began to fade away and it no longer appealed to him, Bill needed to find employment after all he was dating now. Had to maintain his status around the young ladies. On weekends he would gather his buddies and head for the skating rink. That is where the ladies were and the young men as well. Bill would have a problem holding jobs, but for long. There would be Dutch Boy Grocery, Melbourne Iron, and General Electric to name a few. After spending a lot of time at the rink Bill would finally find the woman of his dreams. A beautiful blonde named Joan. Now it was time for the interrogation of his entire life. Bill passes and leaves her grandma captivated by his looks, wit and of course his charm and all through Kathleen's life that would never change.

Bill and Joan dated for a year when Bill asked Joan to marry him. Of course she said yes. Before they could marry she had to change her religion and her second name from Beatrice to Marie due to the Catholic Religion. My mom and dad were married in September 1952 at the Church Of Our Lady in Guelph, Ontario. Bill and Joan were embarking on a long and loving relationship until the end of time. It Sounded like a fairy tale, until it wasn't. Little did they know that the end of time was lurking just around the corner and the pain would go on forever in the hearts of everyone closet to them.

Chapter Seven

After the wedding, Bill and Joan were on their way to Detroit to see their favorite singer Frankie Laine in concert. That was the place they picked for their honeymoon. They would never make it there though because they were in a minor car accident along the way and had to turn back. Now the celebration will have to resume back at their apartment on Herbert Street in Kitchener, Ontario. Finally after several jobs Bill settled in at Kuntz Electroplating, a company our cousins owned. It did not take long for Joan to conceive her first child. His name was Steve was born June 29, 1953. They would pick Clifford as his middle name in remembrance of her brother who was aborted by the hands of her own mother several years earlier. Joan seemed quite content with taking care of her bouncing baby boy, but someone from her past would come back causing more headache and heartache that she tried desperately to put behind her. Opening old wounds of the past is like cutting deeper into the scars that were beginning to finally heal. All she ever wanted was to move past her pain of the past and make beautiful memories for the future. Not asking much you say, well with mommy dearest causing pain and suffering for her daughter I believe gave her such pleasure. She began to invade Joan's new world and I do mean invade…. Bill would nickname her the interfering bitch. She seemed to take pleasure in making anyone's life miserable and unfortunately it would include her grandchildren as well. She especially disliked her oldest granddaughter Joanne.

Two months later Joan would announce that she was expecting again. Everyone seemed pleased, but Bill had concerns. There were rumors of cutbacks at work, but luckily he was able to hang on. Joan was the type of woman when the doctor said the child would be born on a certain date, then that's when it happened to become their first daughter Joanne Marie Schickler, born on May 22, 1954. I was eleven months younger than my older brother. I came 7 days early because mom tripped over Steve's baby bottle. I was to be born on my mother's birthday, hence worth the name Joanne long form for Joan. Bill wanted to name her Joey, but she was not going to have her little girl named with a boy's name. I would grow up my whole life as Joey though.

It was not too long after I was born, work slowed down for dad and he was laid off. With two young children, he needed to find employment immediately. Joan's mother Anna talked with her husband to see about getting a job where he worked. We were moving again which would continue for most of our time with him. We were now off to Guelph, Ontario. We would move in with my mom's worst enemy, her mother. Things were changing within Joan over several months. She was criticized by every move she made. This was the woman who had absolutely no interest in her until she married and had children. We are talking about a young woman who had been mentally abused since her childhood and now mommy dearest is interfering with how she was as a mother and a wife. I wonder to myself, where do you get off? Joan was not a confrontational woman and she did not have the strength to fight back, to stand up for herself ,sadly her downfall. I know she must have felt ashamed to have to go down to a woman who has offered her nothing but pain and agony all her life. Bill was not happy with the circumstances either. As time went by, he would only have contempt for Anna. Sad to say, but I feel the same way.

If things could not get worse, Joan announced she was expecting again. She would give birth to another son named Kenneth William Schickler.

After a year and a half she would deliver another daughter on December 15, 1967. They would name her Lee. It didn't take long for them to find things to do. They were fantastic bowlers and danced beautifully together. They would go to the Canadian Bandstand in Kitchener every Friday night, which was televised the next day so they could watch themselves.

Things were not going well at her mother's place. They would begin to argue a lot and it came down to the only solution was to get out of there. Finally Bill received a call back at Kuntz Electroplating. Joan was the happy one of the two; she could only blossom on her own with no interference from her mother and blossom she did. With four children, it was time for her to seek employment to have something else in her life other than her children. They had a close friend named Ray Boulieau who they bowled with over the years. He informed her that Hager Hinge Ltd. was hiring and he could probably get her a job there. Joan was delighted as well as Bill. It is difficult to say the least to raise four children in one income family. It was quite rare for a woman to work outside the home. She would make friends at work easily. She was still struggling deep down inside she was trying to understand and sort out her emotions concerning her childhood. Her depression consumed her as time went on. If only mommy dearest would remove herself from her life then and only then could she move forward. I do believe at the time Joan had to face the fact her mother adopted a little girl and boy as almost a way to free her own selfish soul for what she did, I could not begin to imagine how she must have felt, the pain, oh... the pain and confusion of feeling she was not wanted and now to have it flaunted in front of her, because I cannot fathom the pain and in later years I guess my mother could not either.

Bill and Joan would spend a lot of time at the Kitchener Hotel and the Walpher. They would meet with friends after bowling. They would consume more alcohol then they should and arguments would ensue. Bill would comment years later that she was an extremely jealous woman and of course dad, a lady's man, was dynamite to their relationship. I think he enjoyed taunting my mother. I remember more times then, I care to, the yelling and screaming of my mother as he beat her. He would storm out the door and back to the pub leaving her alone and crying while he entertained the ladies. That was daddy dearest's way. Everyone commented on the couple and their beautiful children, great jobs, but behind closed doors a storm was brewing out of control. The marriage was deteriorating after ten years and the strain was beginning to show.

As time went by, he would paint the town without her spending their hard earned money impressing other women. Sick really it was important for him to look like the big spender and would buy beers all night. Mom was left alone so much that after a few years it was time to take her children and leave. Why not? She was living alone anyways and the beating continued and did not stop there. His children would be abused in the same manner. It had to eat her up deep inside to watch this monster hurt not only her, but her children too. He was a mean drunk and if you did not watch your words the aftermath was devastating. His children feared him as much as his wife. When he was drunk, the damage he did was like pouring sugar into your gas tank and starting your vehicle. When one of us children did something wrong dad would put us in front of him and ask who did it. When no one responded he would tell us if the person who did this does not come forward all four of us would be subjected to a beating.

As the drinking and beatings continued, she came to the conclusion she must take us and leave. Once again we were moving, this time without dad. There was this wonderful lady Joan worked with that offered her a two bedroom shack where she stored fruit and vegetables. She would clean it out for her and us children. Joan was relieved and Frieda did not charge her a great for it under the circumstances. She waited patiently for the shack as I called it to be finished, and when it was finally done she would have to once again bow down to mother dearest to help her move. That had to be the hardest thing for her to do, but it was for her children. She would pay dearly for it in the months to come. She did not want to go to grandma. She could not stand the embarrassment of letting her think she was a failure. There was also the problem of her grandmother who adored Bill and she could not break her heart with such horrifying details of what she and her children had to endure for years. I remember one particular night when I was awoken by screams in the night and the slamming of the door. I snuck out of the bedroom and into my mom's room. I sat on the bed beside not really understanding why I was even there, but knowing I had too. She hugged me and told me to go back to bed. I remember seeing her wedding dress as I left the room that night. I do not know or understand why it flashes in my mind, maybe something deep down inside told me how much pain that dress has caused her. The year of tears and physical pain she endured and the weakness that was growing in her heart and soul. Would she, could she continue in this manner. Can she even conjure a reason to go on? So many questions so many unanswered. What loneliness must have consumed her, the father/ husband has turned into a monster of many disguises with no regard for the carnage he always left behind. The fear he bestowed upon his wife and children would leave scars on all of them for eternity.

Chapter Eight

The day finally arrived for Joan to move on to a better way of living so she packed up quickly to get us settled in before school ended for the day. The house was not much to look at, but she did her best to make it a home for us. As the mover unloaded the truck an uninvited guest would appear to reclaim his family and I believe she reconciled against her will in fear of any consequences of what would transpire later. If anyone does the walking, it is Bill Schickler and I mean no one else. The drinking and the beatings would continue. Joan was sinking into a dark place and finding it difficult to climb back out. She would reach out, but no one was there to help pull her out. Such sadness clouded her life from the time she was a baby and it was not going to change any time soon.

The shack, that is what I called it, didn't come without problems. We had mice eating our food. Dad would set traps and the next morning he would show us his catch of the day. There were spiders all over the place. I cannot explain why I was so frightened of the place. If Steve was not there when I got home, it did not matter if it was cold or hot, I would not enter until he arrived. He always had a way of making me feel safe and even when we have our ups and downs today, he still does. There would be a huge amount of memories that only he and I shared. I guess that is why no matter the distance he will always be my favorite brother. Our relationship has remained strong regardless of our childish fights. I always knew I could always count on him no matter what we have been through. We both witnessed a tragedy before us and only us. That will always be something we share together. I am thankful for our special memories, for in the not so distant future those memories are all we will have of a place in time that was filled with darkness, and when the sun shone over us, it would never be as bright again.

There were a lot of good times, just too far and in between. I remember and chuckle when we would get home and have a contest eating puffed wheat and seeing if we could finish the handful before mom and dad would get home. We ended up getting caught, but luckily they weren't angry, instead chuckled and said we better eat our dinner. Our father was strict when it came to eating what is put in front of you. One night it was liver and oh... how I hated liver. He would tell me I have to sit there until I finished my plate. So I covered it with ketchup and still I could not muste to swollen another bite. Mom would plead with him to just let me go to bed, but to no avail. I was to sit there and eat it all. Then all of a sudden mom came up pretending to clean the table and she would place pieces of liver from my plate into her apron pockets and smile at me. She had a wonderful smile and her face would glow. I was definitely closer to mom than dad. It may be because my birthday was only 7 days before hers. She was my best friend, my mentor if you will. Kindred spirits you could say. I would not leave her side and never go anywhere with dad without her. I guess in a way, if I could climb back into her womb I would. I put my best friend on a pedestal, and was praying she would not fall off.

The memories are far and in between. I remember when dad and mom would go to the Bridgeport Hotel and leave my brother and I laying in the backseat so no one would see us. One time I remember telling mom I was hungry, she told me to grab an apple from the tree out back. Well all of a sudden I went into crying because a bee has stung me. Mom laughed and made this paste of flour and other ingredients and applied it to the sting. She always made things better with all the love she had. She would sit me in a chair and brush my hair telling me how beautiful I was. I never wanted to leave her side. Dad would tell me many years later that if I could have crawled back into her womb, I would have. I guess I put my mom on a pedestal, but unfortunately she did fall off. I do not think my siblings understand why this tragedy has affected me to this degree. I never was able to move on, that the pain I suffered is as fresh to me as that very night I lost her. I had seven years almost eight of my mom and special moments and of course the oldest daughter. I refuse to apologize for not wanting to let go and keeping this close to me. I knew I was in a moment that was never going to become a form of freedom for me. I am trapped now. The pain and sorrow will never dissipate. Someone special and close to me would tell me to get over it, believe me when I say I have tried, but the person who wants this for me was so much younger at the time of and her memory may not be as lasting as mine or maybe I just can't let go and I doubt I ever will and I will not or cannot be ashamed of that. Mom was my one and only friend and she left me too soon. It is difficult to move on when someone vanishes from your life. A goodbye would have been nice, not much to ask for the lifetime of pain and confusion.

Dad and Steve on the other hand were close. He would spend a lot of time with his oldest son. Practicing, pitching the baseball at Frieda's garage as the target. He could have made it in the big leagues for he had so much power behind every throw. Apparently an injury on his shoulder would crush his dreams of becoming pro. It did not sway him though to try and teach Steve. Maybe he thought he could fulfill his biggest dream through him. We never experienced camping like most families do. But he enjoyed his sports along with my brother. They would watch hockey, baseball, football to name a few. You would think with so much in common they would be inseparable, but something deep down inside of him was lacking compassion, understanding and love. He was a hard man to love, and a charmer at the same time. Was this something he lacked as a child? I guess no one will ever know for sure what was going on in his heart and soul. He would turn out to be someone I would have liked as a friend, but never a father. He treated his friends better than his children and would continue throughout his time on earth, sad really actually quite pitiful, if you ask my opinion. Our father would disappear for four years after the tragedy that awaited us was complete.

The hardest part of writing this book is trying to pull so many memories when they were fogged over with such tragedy heading our way. There would be no warning signs, to comprehend what was being displayed in front of you, sadness, a broken heart that can never mend and be complete again. It is handed to you this way and you will spend the rest of your life trying to make sense of something which is beyond your reach and understanding. But yet you must go on, never to be complete again. It will haunt you and destroy you, if you fall victim to it.

I remember in my heart of memories coming home one day from school. I could hear music as I approached the door. So I quietly walked to the door to see what was going on. There was mom dancing with Uncle Billy . She moved so beautifully and she heard me chuckle. She told me to come in and we danced together. It will always be my favorite memory, I was not left with a lot, but I savor every moment. I am sure that my brother has his own memories locked deep down inside of him. They are more than likely something I do not know, but he has them too. Our younger siblings were so much younger than us, which sometimes I wish I was them. The pain may not have been as devastating as it is. The memory would not be as strong and the loss so great.

On February 9, 1962 my mother and best friend committed suicide in a two bedroom shack that was to give her a new beginning, but instead it was a tragic ending. It began that very morning when she informed her friend Frieda that she would not need a ride to work anymore.

Mom left work early that day with a vial of cyanide tucked neatly in her pocket. She stopped for a few drinks at the Walper Hotel in Kitchener, Ontario before heading home. No one was clear on what time she departed from work and the hotel. When she arrived home, she would be alone.' That was her intention, she somehow lost time as she sank deeper and deeper into the pit of darkness that has casted a shadow on her, her entire life. Her whole miserable life would now flash in front of her as she watched in dismay, there was nothing for her to grab onto or find importance in her life that was worth living for. How horrible it must have been to feel that empty inside. One might say..... Mom was beyond the pain now and slipped into a place she felt she belonged. She spent her whole life in that place, it was all she knew.

No one could begin to fathom the emptiness inside let alone the battle that formed inside her, all her life. I guess in the end my mother lost. Mom would take a child with her. She was 3 months pregnant. Was it the pressure of another child being introduced to a life of hell? No one will ever know. The loss doubled in less than a few hours. The challenge was yet to come for her children. Later on in life the quilt would consume me, haunted with pain and confusion. The quilt, if I would have gotten home earlier, could I have had the power to stop it? The pain, a tremendous loss in my life and finally the confusion: Why? Those ingredients that were placed in me will never go away for the rest of my life. All I could do now is to learn not only how to live without her, but to also learn how to deal with the emptiness she has left behind in me. The hardest part was to deal with the loss of both parents in one night. Our lives will be forever changed for several years to come. We now have become the burden of our relatives on both sides of the family.

Chapter Nine

I t was a cold morning in February of 1962 when I awoke and found I was leaving grandpa's house and off to a new home. He decided to take me out for some pumpkin pie before my journey to a new world was about to begin. I remember sitting across from him and he told me to be careful when ordering pumpkin pie because sometimes they will cheat you and use squash. I listened as he went on. After consuming the pie and light conversation, we proceeded back to the house. Grandpa and I were extremely close. I was his favorite. He never once called me Joanne or Joey, a name I grew up with my entire life. It was Joanie after my mom. He adored my mother so much. Joanne was my given name but was never used by my family, it was always Joey. Dad would say that is the name he wanted me to have, but mom refused so they compromised on it. I remember being five to seven years old and sitting at the table in the basement playing card games with our adult relatives and proud to say I could hold my own. Our family has always been into card games since I could remember.

Grandpa would take me out in the backyard to help pick raspberries and strawberries and tell me to eat a few and not get caught. We were all close to grandpa and visited regularly and I enjoyed it so much. But soon that would be just another memory locked once again deep into my heart, another loss if you will for some time to come.

I remember sitting at the kitchen table silent. I had just watched sadly my entire family dismantle and there was nothing I could do but witness the loss every time one would say goodbye. There has to be a way to correct the carnage adults keep leaving behind for us. I thought please we will not cause trouble and ask for nothing in return to keeping us together. The loss is mounting and there was nothing to do but watch in horror as they left one by one. The loss was not already too great in the last couple days that we have to relive it all over again? Why? Please I just want off of this roller coaster ride and feel happy again, asking too much maybe?

Then came the knock on the door, I was the last wounded child to go. There stood the man I called dad waiting to dump me off to a relative too. When I got into the car I asked him where I was going. He commented on my Uncle Lloyd and Aunt Eleanor's home. The rest of my last ride with my father was in complete silence. I had questions but that did not concern him in the least. It was just another day for him and a devastating one for all my siblings and he was wandering into his own adventure and sadly we were not about to interfere with his plans. They say he went to Calgary to grieve for my woman.

I thought he had part and parcel for putting her where she was and still to this day.

As we approached the driveway to what I would now call home, I could not help but wonder why no one would share what my future had in store for me, when will I see him again if ever, to erase the fear settling into my stomach. Who are these relatives of mine? Have I met them before? What are they like? Do they have children? Will they like me? But the questions answered or not would not take away the loneliness that was brewing deep down inside of me. I just wanted to scream out no daddy please don't leave me here. Please take me with you, but sadly I remained quiet trying to be brave even though I had no idea what was awaiting me behind that big front door. I could only pray for a new beginning.

Then on Esson Street in Kitchener, Ontario the door opened and I met the most wonderful Aunt and Uncle I could have ever dreamed of meeting would become my source of living now. I remember standing in the hallway with my dad's oldest brother looking up at my dad hoping it would register to him. I did not want him to go, but when a person with a heart such as his is as cold a winter's storm there is no way of warming it. That unfortunately was his choice or maybe he entered this world with it, whatever the reason a person cannot feel pain, love, caring understanding and just downright responsibility, what is left? Too not have all of that and more you are not alive anymore, only existing a piece of flesh if you will. Now that to me would be hell on earth. What could have been so devastating in this man's world could have turned him into a life of such uselessness not even experiencing love in his life such emptiness and loneliness I cannot even begin to understand how that must feel. I certainly hope I never will.

The house was huge. As I stood there waiting to see the next step in my scenario my father said goodbye moving my shaking hand to drop to my side and just like the wind he was gone the impact of the loss of my mom, my three siblings and now the creator of our demise my father. Damn right I was scared, lonely, confused and most of all out of place. This was to be my new home now and I would have to make the best of it. I had this wonderful couple and with a bonus of new brothers and sisters to share my life with. Could not be that bad I thought to myself knowing at a young age things could change and without batting an eye, it was all I knew.

So now I will not pull any punches as to why I ended up with the best second parents a young girl could ask for, but in honesty my Aunt, a beautiful woman stepped up to the plate and exercised her religious beliefs, took me in for she is and always will be my godmother. It was her obligation after my father and her brother-in-law abandoned me. I would never fault her for doing what she was obligated to, I admired her for her dedication and strength to bring a child into her home and love me unconditionally. Now that is one hell of a woman. May God Bless Her

Beautiful Soul a woman with unwavering morals, then on the other side my Uncle Lloyd my Rock Hudson I would call him. A heart and soul of pure gold it pains me but yet at the same time, it makes me proud to say, this man was the best dad I have ever had and thank God for allowing me to feel so loved and cared for by these two amazing people.

A moment or two passed by as we stood in the hallway when my Aunt took me upstairs to show me where I would sleep for this day forward. I would share a room with my new sisters MaryAnn and Jane. Across the hall would be my brothers Mark, Thomas, and David. In a few hours their family had grown from six to eight, another to feed to provide for in every sense of the word. There was a roof over my head, a warm bed to sleep in, my tummy was full and all the understanding and love an unwanted child could possibly have. I needed nothing. It could not have been easy to take this challenge on but they did and without batting an eye.

It was now February 12, 1962 when they laid my mother to rest. I was not allowed to attend, which my father forbade me to go and to decide that for me. I had the right to say goodbye, that was stolen from me and through the years it would have a devastating effect on helping me to let her go. I heard once that love was delayed pain, and thinking about it I do agree we will always lose our loved ones, but not being allowed the right to say goodbye is more punishment than death itself don't you agree? So there I was alone confused because my mother would now officially vanish from my existence without as much as a goodbye, the love was gone, like the wind or a winter storm and waiting for the calm once again.

Soon everyone arrived home from the funeral and everything was like nothing happened. I remember sitting there and mom gave me some Valentine's cards to give out to my classmates. I was not sure what they were for. It was my first time. I found one special one in the whole book and I remember writing to my mom. Years and treasures lost time forgotten nothing but sorrow. What I would give to have that card today or anything to remind me, she was my greatest mom.

I do not know precisely how long it took before I was referring to them no longer as Aunt and Uncle, but to Mom and Dad. When I reminisced that I didn't struggle or hard to switch, it seemed natural to me. My sweet cousins would become brother and sisters now. I only prayed that it would last. The overwhelming feeling of finally me in a safe place to try and put the horrible ordeal of the last three days behind me to find peace in my broken heart and my tarnished soul. It burns to this day never to really free me once and for all .I may move on physically but mentally was going to be my life sentence for a crime I did not commit. One forced upon without hesitation to the consequences bestowed upon me and my siblings. Actions some would say,and I have heard this will make you stronger. What? Are you kidding me? Stronger, it will take a lifetime just to comprehend it all and sort it out so your mind can feel the freedom of all this that has cost us internally, psychologically and emotionally. It's a journey if by choice I would not want to take but life is full of twists and turns, you never know what awaits you around the next curve do we? Funny, when I think of my father I do not think of him as my dad. He never really took the time to earn that position in my life. Looking at my last statements above he would reply with It is all a part of growing up. That statement will be forever edged into my memory and how distasteful it is for the rest of my days.

Okay, shall we move on? I seemed to fit in well with my new family. They gave me some ice skates I remember and lessons to boot. I became a member of the Brownies. I remembered on the weekends, mom and dad cleaned the offices at the Brewers in Kitchener, Ontario to make ends meet. One day I asked mom if I could go and help. She seemed pleased and it became a ritual for me. I enjoyed those special moments and I will treasure them. Sad to think that this time and place in my life were my happiest moments and my greatest memories. The only time I had pure happiness and love. There would be a tremble in the foundation of this perfect home, a foundation of complete disapproval of my father's behavior with mom. There were times he showed up to see me come to think about it maybe twice. Mom would not take a back seat and sit idle while he manipulated everyone around him. I remember sitting at the top of the stairs as she berated him for his lack of responsibility as a father. For abandoning his children, but the disgusting part not offering any financial assistance for the care they had given me. She would ask him to buy me a winter coat but it landed on deaf ears. This man literally did absolutely nothing to provide for me and also none of my other siblings. What do you refer to a man such as him? Another question remains, who the hell does he think he is?

I remember crying in silence trying to get a grip on this what he would call fatherly love, but I tried to feel it and begged to feel his love, but came to the realization he is a man without conscience, it has to be the only conclusion. Most people would comment on a dead beat father, some with words that should not be included in my story, but deserved to say at the least. It was only a winter coat, not a major cost especially when you take a moment and calculate how much of their family resources they had put into my care. The love was free.

Pulling memories especially mine at quite a younger age but as you can see I am managing. One was a hot day in Kitchener and I was walking home from school when I heard someone calling out Joey. I looked around to focus on who it was. Not many referred to me as Joey, but my immediate family. Long and behold it was my father who I had not seen in some time. Too busy or not interested we did not talk much. It was hi, how are you and with a blink in the eye another broken promise of coming to see me and then gone again. I rushed home as fast as I could to tell mom that I saw my dad. She really did not have much to say considering the whole situation with my father. She knew deep down inside and I felt it too. He magically appeared though at my Holy Communion at our Catholic Church and would take me for a day visit. There I would meet the woman who was having an affair with my father when my mom was still alive. The woman who helped in destroying my mom along with my world was able to charm her way or rather worm her way in to infest our lives. She was a beautiful woman, I could see why my father was infatuated with an upcoming model in the making. It would seem that upcoming was as far as she achieved.

Dad walked me into her home and I sat at her kitchen table. I remember it well surprisingly, maybe because nightmares last forever. She said hello and handed me a rose from her garden. I thanked her. She had a light lunch and soon I was home where I belonged. I remember mom asking if I had a nice time and to this day I am not sure what I had said. Two simple words and not a one registered or maybe not worth remembering at all. Time would move on and that would just become another memory. I continued staying with mom and dad. I often wondered what was the whole purpose of this little visit? I saw no logical reasoning on constantly bouncing back and forth into my life. Nothing seemed to be gained by it. This would be my last visit for a very long time. My life continued on as though it never happened with dashes of hello and goodbye became a way of life and unfortunately I guess in my heart of hearts came acceptance and not voluntarily. So confused not understanding one nagging questions I would ask myself time to time. Where do I belong? Who am I? How will this affect the choices I make for the future? Has the mold my parents created become my mold too? Will I ever escape this madness forced upon me? No answers will come for what almost feels like an eternity but they did and always will.

That night I crawled into bed and slept as though there was no longer a care in the world. My life would continue in the morning and this visit would just be exactly that, a visit. Not something to fuss about or even mention. Just a flash in my head or memory if you were the one I held deep inside of the loss of mom and my siblings. I longed to be with them. To play like we used to, sit a table together to be a family again. It just was not in the cards not meant to be. I hope one day we would meet again and hopefully get the opportunity to get to know each other or a pipe dream? I was praying not. Time is the only force in making such dreams of mine come true.

In the years that followed my father would re appear, he seemed to have an art of popping in and out. I tried to make sense of why he felt the need to continue his madness of spreading pain and grief to all around him. I was home from school with the measles and laying in the living room on the couch. Mom had put gloves on my hands to avoid me from scratching. She would take my temperature from time to time and make sure I had my fluids. She was a sweet caring and loving woman.

As I was watching television when mom announced I had a visitor. I was so excited wondering who it could be. It did not take for me to recognize the voice. Daddy dearest was back and brought the same red haired woman I met a few years prior. Her name was Agatha. She approached me and knelt down and said. I am going to be your new mommy. The words hit me like no other word has ever done before. Wait a minute, slow it down a new mommy? I already have a mommy in the kitchen. Then it seemed within minutes they were gone as I laid there wondering is this for real or a figment of my imagination? I would pray for it to be so.

That figment would soon become my reality. Probably a week or so later mom asked all the children to go outside except for me. Mom asked me to sit beside her at the kitchen table. I remember sitting there anxious to know what she had to say. Why would she ask everyone to leave? What secret was I about to be told? Then she began to speak. As I looked into her eyes a question popped up. How would I like to go and live with my father? There it was. I responded with yes not knowing what answer was the right one and within moments our conversation was over.

Dad would arrive home from work and he put me on his lap and said he heard I was leaving and I replied yes I am going to be living with my dad. I remember a tear rolling down my cheek and she as he said I would be missed dearly. I had spent 4 wonderful years with a family who cherished and loved more than anyone in my entire life and now it would be gone. Mom and dad would become Aunt and Uncle again but the memories will always remain fresh in my heart forever.

In the days that followed mom bought me a new dress to meet the same man who destroyed my life four years ago who allowed me to be loved by others to lose it for good. The flight was booked and I was saying my goodbyes. I remember looking back before I boarded the plane with tears in my eyes and to this day those tears will return over and over again. Another loss was becoming unbearable. No one could have been aware that I was on my journey back to the Lion's Den. A place of so much pain and suffering that would become more powerful than the seven years I tried desperately to put behind me. A new life was becoming, but a wonderful life over and one that would impact our lives once again as we sat in horror to relive it all over again.

Joanne Schickler
Copyright 2022